THE LITTLE BOOK OF

STILL

CALM FOR BUSY LIVES

BY

ANNIE HARVEY

In memory of mum.

Your love and laughter lives on in me.

x

Table of Contents

Night

FOREWORD

It was such a great honour when Annie asked me to write the Foreword for this wonderful book. As a published author myself and devotee to the power of the pen, or should I say, keyboard, I was eager to devour every word and ponder the importance of the message. In anticipation of reading the Little Book of Still, I prepared myself for the tough questions that were already bubbling up, 'Was I as calm and calibrated within myself and within my life that I wanted to be, or believed myself to be? Or worse, was this going to be a moment where I would have to confront, with deep honesty, the increasing allowance I was giving to the 'creep' of the outside 'noise' into my mind?

Annie's voice whispered gently from the first page - telling me that this seemingly small book was in fact a very big reminder that no one is too busy to find the time and space to just stop, to breathe, to see, to hear, and vitally to listen to one's self.

I've been involved in the practice of Mindfulness for many years, I write and speak about the power of the mind, how our thoughts determine our actions and why it is 'difference making' to be conscious and aware of our every thought. It is truly transformational. I know, because I've used this knowledge to literally rebuild my life after surviving the atrocity of a deliberate action of a suicide bomber who targeted an under-ground train on one of London's busy commuter routes.

In the time it takes to draw a single breath, my life and those around me changed forever. I survived the initial blast, although I wasn't expected to live due to the horrific nature of my injuries, mainly losing both of my legs.

The early memory of waking up in hospital and being unable to move any part of my body except my eyes is still as vivid as the reality was, now just over ten years ago.

This was my moment of revelation - this was my true, first understanding of what I was capable of, how I could transform my position by choosing how I wanted to react and respond. I could be in control of what appeared to be an out of control situation *simply* by focussing on the mental benefits of being 'stopped' physically. Whilst my body was in a weakened state, I gave my mind permission to be strong, to help me develop the tools I needed to face, with confidence, all that was 'unknown'.

I believe that we each hold the value and the wisdom of our 'Lived Experience', all the trials and the tribulations that we go through, their effect and their lessons become woven into our very fabric, the 'stuff' that essentially influences and shapes who we are. It's in my moments of complete Still, that I reflect upon this incredible asset, how everything I need, I have, it's all inherently there, waiting.

Thank you Annie for reminding me of the brilliance that lays within us all, that we don't need a tragedy to gain a greater respect for our wondrous self and for highlighting what we do that may seem like small gestures can actually lead to BIG, positive and life affirming change.

Dr Gill Hicks AM MBE

INTRODUCTION

Ah, the irony! As I turn on my computer to write these, the very first words of this book, it tells me it is 'updating', and I will have to wait. And it takes quite a while!

So, what do we do when this happens in our busy lives? When we are made to wait by forces outside of our control? Walk away? Leave it? Find something else to busy ourselves with? Sit and feel frustrated?

Or, do we see this as a perfect opportunity for a little pause in our lives, a 'pattern interrupt'. Do we turn the inconvenience on its head, consider it a gift, and use the time wisely because, really, when was the last time we were just...'still'?

The idea for this little book came about very quickly, following my recent TEDxAdelaide talk. Audience members asked me if there was a book, and I replied, 'Of course there is', because that is what you do when you work for yourself and someone asks you for a service!

And then I came home, sat down, and realised that I had just committed myself to writing a book, quickly, because the other thing you do when you work for yourself is never let your customers down!

So, I started writing, and the funny thing is, it came naturally, like I was always intended to write a funny little book about being calm! And here it is!

On November 2nd, 2017, I stood on the famous red dot and talked to 1,000 people: people who were all there to hear new ideas and have their paradigms shifted, just a little.

15 brave and extremely nervous men and women, driven by the passion for their chosen topics, many of whom had never spoken in public before, stood up one by one and gave such energy and honesty to their words that any hesitation, stuttering or

forgetfulness was immediately forgiven. The whole room supported them and roared their approval.

I was one of them. The timing of who spoke when was worked out in fine detail. I was 2nd on, after supper. I was on after Sue. Sue had a topic which was going to be confronting for many. I would be known as the 'circuit breaker'.

Circuit Breaker: an automatic device for stopping the flow of current in an electric circuit as a safety measure."

Or was I in fact a 'Pattern Interrupt'?

Pattern Interrupt: a technique to change a particular thought, behaviour or situation.

Either way, my positioning appeared to have a purpose!

My talk was short (under 6 minutes) and intended to be 'easy to digest'; I didn't want my audience ruminating, but instead quickly moving on to making positive change. The topic was anxiety and my aim was to connect science behind it with the internal resources we all already have to cope with it.

And, it worked! 1,000 people listened and then laughed! More importantly, lots of them have been in touch with me since to say they are actively using and sharing the exercise I taught them! Woo hoo!

A twenty-five-year old has written since to say she's been using it every day to deal with her stress; a father of four in the audience said he was taking it home to his children as it was so simple yet effective; a mother told me it was a reminder to look after herself first.

My message needed to go further. So, this little book is for everyone who thinks that they are too busy to meditate, too busy to stop, even more a moment, and make time for themselves. It is for everyone that needs a 'pattern interrupt'.

The exercise I taught at TEDxAdelaide, The STILL Effect, is provided in this book on page 57. Try it, repeat it, share it!

This book is full of very quick strategies that you can use throughout your day, each no longer than 3 minutes. That's right, you can start improving your mental health in less than 3 minutes! I've also included my favourite quotes to inspire you too.

The book is also in no particular order, so you start at the beginning and work to the end or just pick a page at random and have a go! I have put them into 3 sections of Morning, Noon and Night but really you can try them all at any time. This is intentional, because the tricky part is convincing yourself that you have time to do this, that it's okay to focus on yourself for a few minutes and not worry about the needs of others.

A common criticism of books on mindfulness is the focus on theory first and practical application later. It is a criticism that I have levelled myself many times. Like the rest of you, I'm busy, and I want my aspirin now, I don't want to ready the scientific theory behind it, I just want my headache to go away! The Small Book of Still is designed to give you back some control straight away.

Please bear in mind, though, that the criticism can work in reverse. The quick tools provided in this little book are a toe in the water compared to the big pond that is mindfulness. I have been swimming in its waters for years now, and I still find hidden depths and little inlets to explore.

*"Each morning we're born again
of yesterday nothing remains
what's left began today."*

- Palladas

GOOD MORNING!

It's a brand new day.

Time to begin again.

Before you get out of bed, bring your attention to your breathing.

Observe the feeling of just five mindful breaths.

That's it!

Then move on with your day.

Annie Aide (French for help)

When I wake up a bit 'low', I add a big grin to my face. It's amazing how your mood can change instantly!

"The little things?
The little moments?
They aren't little."

on Kabat-Zinn

PUT THE KETTLE ON

A watched kettle never boils, right?

We all know the phrase, and it makes perfect sense. You're wasting time, get on with something more useful until it's boiled! Guilty?

But what if something that we think of as time wasting could in fact be useful in its own right?

Let's call it the Kettle Meditation.

First, switch the kettle on.

Then, just stand there, watching, because of course a watched kettle *does* in fact eventually boil.

Take a long deep breath. Notice what's going on inside your body. Permission granted to let the world turn without you for a few moments.

Think of it as a mini-break from all the doing in your busy life. It's a hectic world out there and you deserve a little time off every now and then. Yes you.

In the words of Zen Master Thich Nhat Hanh, think of the kettle as a "bell of mindfulness,". Feel your feet on the floor and take a long deep breath. Take another long deep breath.

Then relax and smile as you pour your tea and move on with your day a little more gently.

Annie Aide

When I teach mindfulness meditation, I often invite attendees to use this 'kettle' time as their intro to finding some 'time' to start practising formal mediation, even if for just a few seconds.

"Tea is an act complete in its simplicity.
When I drink tea, there is only me and the
tea. The rest of the world dissolves."

Thích Nhất Hạnh

WARM DRINK, WARM HEART

Make yourself a cup of your favourite tea.

Sit comfortably.

Cup it in your hands.

Feel the warmth.

Lean over, close your eyes and smell the aroma.

Lift the cup with both hands and take a small mouthful.

Taste the flavour.

Enjoy the moment, then swallow slowly, enjoying the sensation of it moving down your throat.

Repeat until finished. Prescribe at least one a day for a personal pause and reflection.

Annie Aide

I do this every day at our local café with my first coffee of the day.

"Do not waste a single moment."
This is my principle.
Therefore, my daily life is extremely busy.
However, that is how I feel joy."

Kyoshu Sama

SHOWER TIME

We could say that mindfulness is 'coming to our senses'. We bring our full attention to what our body is feeling, seeing, hearing, tasting and smelling. In other words, noticing everything the present moment offers to our senses.

By getting 'out of your head' and coming to our senses, we leave behind the stories our thoughts are telling us and we arrive at a more direct experience of what is happening 'in the now'.

Have you ever got out of the shower and asked yourself the question 'Did I just wash my hair?' This is because we've been on autopilot.

Having a shower is the perfect opportunity to turn an everyday, and often forgotten, experience, in to a mindful activity. Try it.

Turn on the shower. Feel the water on your hand as you wait for the temperature to be just right. Feel its texture, the way it moves across your skin.

Now extend this experience to your entire body as you step in, feeling the water fall on you.

Feel your skin taking in moisture.

Listen to the water..

Close your eyes and let yours senses take over.

As you use your soap and shampoo, take note of the feel of it, the smell.

More than most meditations, the shower meditation is enhanced by a physical separation from the 'real' world

Annie Aide

Even just 30 seconds of your three minute shower can make all the difference.

"There is something wonderfully bold and liberating about saying yes to our entire imperfect and messy life."

Tara Brach

SLOW FOOD

Whenever you eat or drink something, take a minute and breathe. When do we really savour what we're eating? Treat one meal a day like it's the most exquisite thing you've ordered on a menu.

Look at your food and appreciate that the food was connected to something that nourished its growth.

Pay attention as you eat, bringing awareness to seeing, smelling, tasting, chewing, and swallowing your food. Slow each step down and notice all the sensations.

Try it with your own favourite, even if just for the first mouthful.

Leave the table refreshed and ready for the next part of your day.

Annie Aide

I do this every morning with my first few mouthfuls of breakfast. My personal favourite is eating passion fruit, which has become a regular mindful meditation for me, adding to my appreciation of this wonderful fruit.

You can also try it with your first glass of wine in the evening!

"Walk as if you are kissing the Earth with your feet."

Thích Nhất Hạnh

WALK WITH ME

Become aware of everything in your body as you walk.

Notice how the ground feels under your feet, your breath as you move, what you can see and hear around you, how quickly you are walking.

Use walking as an opportunity to slow down or let go of anything. Even better, remove your shoes and socks and walk on grass, feeling that intimate connection with the earth and becoming truly 'grounded'.

Repeat wherever you can; the beach, your back garden, a forest, even a park or car park during your lunchbreak.

"You are the sky.
Everything else is just the weather."

Pema Chödrön

RED LIGHT

How often do we say, I'd love to have time to stop and smell the roses, but life is too busy? Yet when we do get some rare time to ourselves, we either miss the opportunities or don't know what to do with them.

Think about traffic lights. Finally, an opportunity to stop, but do we enjoy it? Probably not, because we see it as an inconvenience, and not an opportunity to practice mindfulness and give ourselves a brief rest.

It takes a simple shift in attitude to transform the way we experience these unexpected frustrations.

So, let's change it. Use this brief opportunity to relax back in your car seat. Become aware your breath. Allow your shoulders to drop. Notice your environment, inside and outside; the sounds, the people, the colours, the weather.

And then, once the light has turned green, you can proceed with your journey feeling relaxed and rejuvenated.

Annie Aide

I like to encourage my husband to do this when he's driving!

*"If you aren't in the moment,
you are either looking forward to uncertainty,
or back to pain and regret."*

Jim Carrey

VITAL SIGNS

Take several normal breaths in and out. Notice where you feel your breath. Where is it?

Chest? Belly? Nose? Ribcage? Mouth? Throat?

Often when we are tense, our breath is in our upper chest. Can you see if you can instead move it to your belly, so that your belly rises before your chest? (see Breathing Bears)

Paying attention to our breath is a way of anchoring ourselves in the present moment. It is always here for us to return to if our attention drifts off to the future or past. I call it 'coming home'.

As soon as your mind wanders (as it naturally does), we just need to notice that it has wandered and come back to paying attention to your breath.

Begin again. Focus your attention on how it feels, where you notice the air moving, how your chest and abdomen move. You are not looking for a revelation from this experience; think of it more like a little mental push-up for your mind.

"Life is a preparation for the future;
and the best preparation for the future
is to live as if there were none."

Albert Einstein

STOP

The STOP method is a 'mini' meditation, useful for a stressful or difficult moment. It deliberately focuses on the breath, body sensations and present moment experience and this **interrupts us** from being stuck in a cycle of thinking.

S stands for 'stop'

Stop what you're doing and open your attention wide, taking in everything that's happening right now.

T stands for 'take a deep breath'

Take a slow deep breath, and as you do so, tune into the sensations of breathing. Gather your attention and hone in on the exact sensations of breathing right now in this moment. Be as present as you can with the full journey of the breath into and out of the body.

O for 'observe'

Observe your body and emotions. What sensations can you feel in your feet, legs, head, arms and shoulders? Then widen your focus and open to what is happening in the environment around you. What can you see, feel, smell, hear or taste?

You have, quite literally, come to your senses!

P for 'proceed'

Proceed with what you were doing with the intention of integrating this mindful awareness into your daily activity.

Annie Aide

This is often the favourite of my clients as it's so easy to remember!

"In today's rush, we all think too much —
seek too much —
want too much —
and forget about the joy of just being."

Eckhart Tolle

MINDFUL MOBILE

A really quick one, to be practised every day.

Before answering that call, simply take 2 deep breaths before answering.

You may be surprised by the immediate effect of this little exercise; the person on the other end might even comment how calm you sound!

Annie Aide

I always do this one. Even I notice the tone of my voice changes on answering.

"Do not dwell in the past,
do not dream of the future,
concentrate the mind
on the present moment."

Buddha

MINDFUL INTERRUPTIONS

Try to see an interruption in your day as an opportunity for a mindful moment.

You are working quietly in your office when you hear rubbish truck outside. You are deep in thought waiting for a train when an announcement comes over the speakers. You are walking along a road when you hear a siren.

Take a deep breath.

Take stock of what you are thinking, how you are feeling and what you are doing.

Continue with your day.

Annie Aide

I always do this when the next door neighbour starts to mow the lawn!

"Nothing is as important as this day."

Goethe.

5 THINGS

Notice 5 things in your day that usually go unnoticed and unappreciated.

These could be things you hear, smell, feel, see or touch. For example, focus on a particular colour, yellow perhaps, and try and spot and really notice where that colour appears in your day.

Allow yourself to fall awake in the world and fully experience the environment.

Annie Aide

Great one to do with your children or students. I have also taken a mindful photograph spotting a new colour each day of the week.

"Today, like every other day, we wake up empty and frightened. Don't open the door to the study and begin reading. Take down a musical instrument."

Rumi

MINDFUL DOOR

The moment you touch a door handle, allow yourself to be completely mindful of where you are, how you feel what you are doing.

This may be leaving or returning to your home, entering or leaving your car, at your favourite café or at your office Wherever it is, pause with your hand on the door handle, breathe in deeply and let your senses and thoughts flood in.

Try using this simple everyday act as a 'trigger' to relax and breathe more deeply.

Annie Aide

Mum always said, when one door closes another will open and it's been so true in my life so far...

"You can't stop the waves,
but you can learn to surf."

Jon Kabat-Zinn

THREE-MINUTE MOMENT

There are three steps to this:

1. **Attend to what is.** The first step is to openly observe your experience, noting it, but without the need to change what is being observed.

2. **Focus on the breath.** The second step narrows the field of attention to a single, pointed focus on the breath in the body.

3. **Attend to the body.** The third step widens attention again to include the body as a whole and any sensations that are present.

Each step of the Three-Minute Breathing Moment is roughly one minute in length.

Annie Aide

My mum had Alzheimer's. When she was repeating the same story for the tenth time, I would listen like I had heard it for the first time, whilst doing this Three Minute Moment Activity.

"Treat everyone you meet
as if they were you."

Doug Dillon

4-7-8 BREATHING

In times of stress, you can immediately tame the 'fight-or-flight' response misfiring in your brain, cool your body's inflammatory response to all those stress hormones, and *halt anxiety or panic* by using a simple breathing technique.

I recently learned this technique from a friend who is a counsellor. I find it really helpful when I am feeling irrationally worried or anxious.

The technique is called **4-7-8 Breathing**, and it has five easy steps:

1. Place the tip of your tongue against the roof of your mouth, right behind your front teeth.

2. Breathe in through your nose for a count of 4.

3. Hold your breath for a count of 7.

4. Release your breath from your mouth with a whooshing sound for a count of 8.

5. Without a break, breathe in again for a count of 4, repeating the entire technique 3-4 times in a row, then resume normal breathing and activity.

If you use a second hand on a watch to count your breaths, the whole exercise will take just 57 seconds! But it doesn't really matter if each count lasts an actual second; it only matters that you *count evenly* so the ratio of 4-7-8 is maintained.

You may find yourself feeling mildly light-headed after doing this. That's actually a sign it is working, and it will quickly pass. Feel free to do this as often as you want, but you may need to get used to it first.

Annie Aide

This does take quite a bit of practise. It's a good one for anxiety but make sure you're feeling calm when you first learn it before putting it into action when you really need it most.

"If you clean the floor with love,
you have given the world
an invisible painting."

Osho

FEET FIRST

One way to develop skills to effectively deal with strong emotions is by using the soles of our feet, helping us to quickly calm down and resist the urge to act out. Hmm ring a bell?

The purpose is to quickly shift our attention away from something that may have triggered us to a neutral grounding point in the body— the soles of the feet. This in turn has a calming effect on the body, and the attention is diverted.

1. If you are standing, stand in a natural posture, with the soles of your feet flat on the floor. If you are sitting, sit comfortably with the soles of your feet flat on the floor.
2. Breathe naturally, and do nothing.
3. Now, shift all your attention to the soles of your feet.
4. Slowly, move your toes, feel your shoes covering your feet, feel the texture of your socks, the curve of your arch, and the heels of your feet against the back of your shoes. If you do not have shoes on, feel the floor with the soles of your feet.
5. Keep breathing naturally and focus on the soles of your feet until you feel calm.

Practice this until you can use it wherever you are and whenever an incident occurs that may lead to you being aggressive and acting out. Remember that once you are calm, you can walk away from the situation with a smile on your face because you controlled your anger.

Annie Aide

This is particularly useful when someone is right in front of you and triggering you. You can still be present with them and calm whilst focussing on your feet.

"That's life: starting over,
one breath at a time."

Sharon Salzberg

ONE BIG BREATH

At any time during the day, take a moment to focus on your breath.

Take one slow breath.

Breathe in as slowly as possible while thinking, "I am."

Then, exhale just as slowly, and think, "at peace."

Repeat as needed until the tension starts to melt.

Stress is often behind us or in front of us, and not actually here and now. Breathing pulls you into the present.

*"Be happy in the moment, that's enough.
Each moment is all we need, not more."*

Mother Teresa

SOUND ONLY

Listen to the sounds around you for a few seconds to a few minutes.

Be like a microphone, absorbing the sounds and their tone and vibrations.

Note the things you hear coming in and out of your awareness.

Do this at different places like work and home, on public transport, at the shops.

Annie Aide

I love this one! Life is full of noise. Even our thoughts are noise, just noise.

*"The moment one gives close attention
to anything,
even a blade of grass,
it becomes a mysterious,
awesome,
indescribably magnificent world in itself."*

Henry Miller

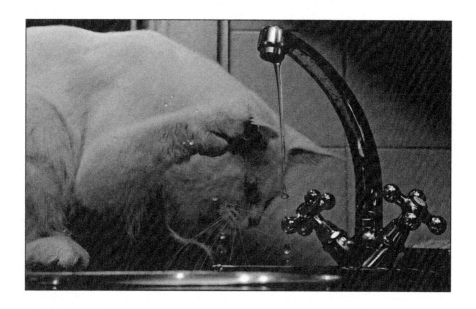

SOAP

Think about how many times you might wash your hands during the day. Use this as a moment to be present.

Turn on the water and hold your hands under the tap until the temperature is just right for you.

Listen to the water as it falls across your hands and then down to the sink.

Add some soap to your hands and lather gently and mindfully.

Feel your fingers moving, feel the soap on your skin.

Take in the smell of the soap before washing the lather away.

Dry your hands slowly.

Carry on with your day.

"I exist as I am - that is enough;
If no other in the world be aware,
I sit content."

Walt Whitman.

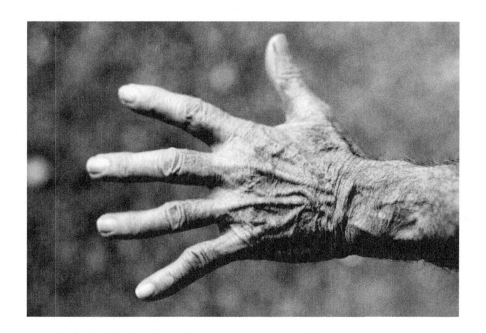

HANDS OUT

Our hands are excellent objects of meditation. With over 1 billion nerve endings each, there is a vast array of sensation in our hands that is constantly showing us the present moment.

Take a moment to notice your hands right now, and experience the power of a hand meditation:

- Allow your hands to rest, in your lap, on your knees, or wherever feels comfortable.
- Bring your attention into your hands and simply notice the sensations.
- Notice any pain or discomfort, opening to those sensations without resistance, allowing them to be as they are.
- Notice the pulsing and tingling inside your hands.
- Notice the feeling of the air passing over the skin.
- Notice the textures of any surfaces that your hands are touching.
- Notice the sense of warmth or coolness.

- Now, holding one hand gently in the palm of the other, look closely at it.
- Notice all the details.
- Reflect upon how much your hands have done for you over the course of your life.
- Rest in awareness of these sensations in your hands, feeling a sense of gratitude for them.

Even briefly checking in with your hands in this way can be a great way to reconnect with the moment throughout your day. By being aware of the sensations in your hands with care and appreciation, regular daily activities such as holding the steering wheel, washing the dishes can become frequent and enjoyable practices of mindfulness.

Annie Aide

It's easier to find sensations in our hands or feet when first starting to practise formal mindfulness meditation. Even if you just shake your hands for 10 seconds and stop, you'll feel something.

I also used to do this with mine and mum's hands, comparing them, often photographing them cooking or sewing together.

"We're so busy watching out for what's just ahead of us that we don't take time to enjoy where we are."

Bill Watterson

54321

You can sit almost anywhere and do this exercise, and it only takes a few minutes.

Find somewhere comfortable to sit and take a few mindful breaths.

Notice 5 things you can see. Focus on them closely, each in turn.

Pick out 4 sounds. Again, notice each one individually. Listen closely to them, isolating them from the other noises around you.

Choose 3 things to feel. These could be anything from the clothes you're wearing to your pet or the feel of your chair. Focus on what each one feels like, one at a time.

Choose 2 smells or tastes. These can be ones you're experiencing currently, or those you have a strong memory of. So, you could smell and sip a drink, or remember the taste of something delicious you had earlier in the day. It doesn't matter which, just choose two and zone in on them.

After doing the four parts above, I come back to thinking of all my senses together, my body as a whole, and take one big, deep mindful breath. It always feels fantastic!

Annie Aide

Another great one for the kids!

"The way to live in the present is to remember that 'This too shall pass.'

When you experience joy, remembering that 'This too shall pass' helps you savour the here and now.

When you experience pain and sorrow, remembering that 'This too shall pass' reminds you that grief, like joy, is only temporary."

Joey Green

MINDFUL CHECK IN

1. Choose a natural object from within your immediate environment and focus on watching it for a minute or two. This could be a flower or an insect, the clouds, a candle or the exit sign at work.
2. Don't do anything except notice the thing you are looking at. Simply relax into watching for as long as your concentration allows.
3. Look at this object as if you are seeing it for the first time (some call this a beginner's mind).
4. Visually explore every aspect of its formation, and allow yourself to be consumed by its presence.

*"No one has ever been angry
at another human being
we're only angry at our story of them."*-

Byron Katie

ONE MINUTE SENSES CHECK

Sit down in a comfortable position. Finding comfort helps us to pay attention to whether we are hunching over our desks, for example, or sitting at a funny angle.

Sit up straight, close your eyes and take a breath.

Focus in on your senses (or a particular sense). This is a powerful way of bringing your attention to what is around you. Often our homes and offices are busy, and you will hear lots of noises around you, but paying attention to them in a mindful way allows you to become aware of those sounds but not react to them.

Bring your attention to your body and how it is feeling.

Now, return to your breath.

"The most precious gift we can offer others
is our presence.
When mindfulness embraces those we love,
they will bloom like flowers."

Thich Nhat Hanh

MINDFUL LISTENING

When we are listening mindfully, making our hearing the primary sense, we are fully present with what we are hearing without trying to control it or judge it.

We let go of our inner voice and our usual assumptions, and we listen with respect to precisely what is being said.

For all listening to be effective, so we understand and remember what is being heard, we need a mind that is open, fresh, alert, attentive, calm, and receptive.

Our minds are constantly racing ahead to what we're going to say next. We're never 100% in the moment.

We often do not have a clear concept of listening as an active process that we can control, but, in fact, mindful listening can be cultivated through practice.

When in conversation, give the gift of listening. Don't rush ahead to how you're going to respond, just be fully present with the other person. It truly is a gift.

Annie Aide

If you have teenage children or students, try being in the moment and really listen, even just for a few minutes. They will notice, I promise!

"If you want others to be happy,
practice compassion.
If you want to be happy,
practice compassion."

Dalai Lama

KINDNESS

Sometimes we just need to get out of our own way. A good way to do this is to practise a random act of kindness once or twice in your week.

Examples:

Tell a random stranger they look good in their outfit (only if you believe they do of course!)

Hold a door open for someone.

Pay for a coffee for a stranger.

Annie Aide

You may feel uncomfortable doing this, but most people will appreciate it so give it a try!

"The stiller you are the calmer life is."

Rasheed Ogunlaru

STILL

Here's the tool I created and launched at TEDxAdelaide.

Search for Annie Harvey TEDx Adelaide on YouTube.

ST	STOP	STOP, wherever you are, e.g. when you shut your front door, when waiting for the kettle to boil, waiting to cross the road, at the traffic lights or in the shower. Just stop, for a few moments.
I	INHALE	INHALE, and feel the movement of breathing in your body, inhaling and exhaling a few times. Pay attention to breath entering your body. Perhaps notice the pause between your in-breath and your out-breath. Take a mental pause.
L	LISTEN	LISTEN, to the world around you. Just let all the sounds near and far come in and out of your awareness.
L	LAUGH	Finally, LAUGH, out-loud and on-purpose, for 5-10 seconds!

Annie Aide

I still can't believe that I got nearly 1,000 people doing the above at Adelaide Town Hall!

"The real voyage of discovery consists not in seeking out new landscapes but in having new eyes."

Marcel Proust

PASSING CARS

Take 3-4 deep breaths as slow as possible.

Focus on the rise and fall of your chest and belly, noticing the sensations in your body.

Now, let any thoughts you may have come and go in the background, like cars passing.

When a new thought appears, briefly acknowledge its presence like nodding at a passing motorist, but keep focussing on the breath. If any thought hooks you, take a second to notice the hook that distracted you then gently unhook and refocus on breathing.

Practise anytime anywhere.

Annie Aide

I'll let you in to a secret. If you can do above even for a few seconds that is Mindfulness!

"We spend precious hours
fearing the inevitable.
It would be wise
to use that time
adoring our families,
cherishing our friends
and living our lives."

Maya Angelou

TRANSITION

Before getting out of your car after work, shopping etc, sit still for a moment.

Feel your back on the seat, the texture, the warmth, the contours.

Feel your hands on the steering wheel, the grip, the texture.

Feel the sun through the windscreen.

Feel the air.

Tune into your breath for a moment, taking 2 deep breaths.

Note what has gone well so far in your day.

You have given yourself space, a 'transition', between one part of your life and the next.

Annie Aide

I do this regularly before entering my house!

*"This is the real secret of life —
to be completely engaged
with what you are doing
in the here and now.
And instead of calling it work,
realize it is play."*

Alan Watts

BREATHING BEARS

Breathing Bears is one of my favourite mindful breathing exercises for kids. This activity helps learn focusing skills, calm down and figure out that paying attention to our bodies helps us relax.

During this activity with children, put on some soothing music whilst they lie on their backs with a stuffed toy on their bellies.

Their only instruction is to breathe normally and pay attention to the sensation of the toy, feeling it rise and fall as they inhale and exhale.

Belly breathing calms down the nervous system. Addiing a favourite stuffed toy, younger kids will get it almost immediately and find it fun to try out.. Even pre-schoolers can do it!

Another variation is to tell your child to pretend that he rocks the stuffed animal to sleep.

Annie Aide

I do this activity too, sometimes with a book or mobile phone on my belly!

*"My experience is
that many things are not as bad
as I thought they would be."*

Mary Doria Russell

TUNING IN

Mindful music listening can be a wonderful way to reduce your stress and reconnect with your body and breath. Music can help you stay focused, whilst simultaneously providing a source of strength and creative energy.

Take a moment to think about the music in your life. Do you listen to music regularly? Is it live music? Recorded music? What kind of music moves you? Helps you relax? Energizes you? Do you play an instrument or sing? What music do you hear around you?

Now think about your relationship with music for a moment. Is it a source of frustration or a joy? Do you feel disconnected from music sometimes? Does music soothe you when nothing else seems to work? Do you have a lot of music on your phone but never listen to it?

Whether you listen to music all the time or rarely, mindful music listening can help you slow down and be in the moment.

Take a moment to breathe and ground yourself. Inhale and exhale gently. Notice your body, and tune into how it feels whether you're standing, sitting, walking, or lying down

Then, listen. Use headphones or earbuds if that helps you focus or shut out external noise. Give yourself permission to only listen to the music, without simultaneously checking your email or refreshing your Facebook feed.

Let yourself be aware of anything you notice, without judgment or self-criticism. Notice the pace of the music, the sounds of the different instruments, or the shifts in volume. Notice if you're more aware of a certain part of your body as you listen. Notice any thoughts or feelings that come up—perhaps the music is connected to a memory, or perhaps an anxious thought is trying to pop through. Let any thoughts just pass through your awareness, and then gently bring yourself back to the sounds of the music.

Take a moment to breathe and check in with your body, your breath and your mind. Does anything feel different? Do you notice any shifts after listening to the piece of music? Do you feel calmer?

You may also find that repeating the same piece of music is a sort of touchstone, a way to continually reconnect to that place inside where gentle pausing and noticing can happen with ease.

Annie Aide

I have two pieces of music that I play when I need to privately feel my grief of losing mum.

"The place to be happy is here.
The time to be happy is now."

Robert G. Ingersoll

3 smiles

AND NOW FOR THE SMILES AND LAUGHTER!

3 Smiles is something I have printed on the back on my business cards. It's about practising an attitude of gratitude and I just had to add it to the book as it has given me so much joy.

At the end of each day, think of or write down 3 things that made you smile that day.

This is particularly important if you have had a bad day; don't let your head hit that pillow until you've thought of 3, and they can be REALLY small things!

It is amazing the effect it can have when you flip that glass-half-empty upside down and focus on the positives. It gives your mind a little smile of remembrance and moves your outlook to positive. You will sleep better and feel better about the day that you have just completed.

Repeat every night.

"Don't believe everything you think.
Thoughts are just that - thoughts."

Allan Lokos

SMILEY FACES

Smiling, whether real or fake, sends a message to the brain. Once the brain gets the message, two things happen.

First, it prompts the brain to release 'happiness' chemicals (endorphins).

Second, it creates a 'feedback loop', causing mood-elevating reactions in your body. This even happens if you fake a big grin, and hold it, it just takes a little longer.

In short, however you get there, real or fake, a smile produces chemical changes in your body that literally make you feel better.

So here are some ideas:

- Smile at your reflection in the mirror.
- Start and finish your day with a smile.
- Smile at someone randomly in the street.
- Notice the smiles around you (you may find yourself smiling).
- Practise smiling even when there is nothing to smile about.

BREATHE, STRETCH, SMILE

- Sit or stand, breathe in deeply as you raise your arms above your head, hold for a second then lower and smile as you exhale
- Repeat, inhaling and stretching.
- Get creative with your stretches, let out a gentle chuckle with the exhale if you feel one emerging.

EXAGGERATED YAWNING

- Yawns are a great way to release tension and involve an intake of oxygen, so we may as well enjoy the process.

- Next time you feel a yawn coming on, really exaggerate the movement and sound and finish with a smile and sigh.

HUGGING LAUGH

- Hug yourself (or someone else - with their permission of course) and smile as you start to rock your body softly. When it begins to feel good inside and you notice yourself beginning to relax, start to laugh gently.

"You'll find that life is still worthwhile,
if you just smile.

Charlie Chaplin

SMILING MEDITATION

Take a comfortable pose, sitting or lying down.

Close your eyes, take a deep breath in slowly through your nose, then breath out through your mouth. Do it 1-3 times, until you can put your attention and focus into your body.

Allow a slight smile to come onto your lips. It doesn't have to be big, just until you have the sense that your lips are smiling.

Feel how happy your lips feel.

Now slowly allow the happy feeling to spread over your face.

Bit by bit, allow the feeling of the smile to spread through your body.

Take 3 deep breaths before opening your eyes.

How did it feel?

Annie Aide

Remember you can do this at any time during your day to bring back that feeling.

"Make haste slowly."

Zen saying

THE QUEUE

Whenever you wait in a line, use this time to notice standing and breathing.

Feel the contact of your feet on the floor and how your body feels.

Notice to the rise and fall of your abdomen.

Feel your body as it sways slightly and adjusts to take pressure from one side to the other.

Feel the weight of your arms as they hang at your sides, and your fingers as you flex them slowly.

Perhaps close your eyes for a moment and let your mind count off the different sounds it can hear: breathing, conversations, traffic, air conditioning.

Are you still feeling impatient?

"If you concentrate on finding whatever is good in every situation, you will discover that your life will suddenly be filled with gratitude, a feeling that nurtures the soul."

Rabbi Harold Kushner

GRATITUDE

Take on an attitude of gratitude.

I've been writing my Gratitude Journal for about 7 years. I started with my class of Year 2s putting in marbles each time they made good choices. You know how it goes: full jar at end of the week and free play on Friday afternoon.

I started doing my own 'marble jar' for things that had gone well in my day and things I was grateful for.

It really works!

Annie Aide

Sometimes this is hard to do, in particular if you've had a bad day. Even more reason to do it! Don't let your head hit that pillow until you've written 3 things, however small. My journaling is helped by finding some really beautiful and tactile stationary to journal in.

MORE ON MINDFULNESS

If you are stressed, anxious, tense or worried, mindfulness meditation can help. Spending even a few minutes in meditation can restore your calm and inner peace.

Anyone can practice meditation. It is personal, easy and free, and it doesn't require any special equipment.

You can practice meditation wherever you are, whether you are out for a walk, riding the bus, waiting at the doctor's office or even in the middle of a difficult business meeting.

Understanding Meditation

Meditation has been practiced for thousands of years. These days, meditation is commonly used for relaxation and stress reduction. It is considered a type of mind-body complementary medicine and can produce a deep state of relaxation and a tranquil mind.

Benefits of Meditation

Meditation can give you a sense of calm, peace and balance that can benefit both your emotional well-being and your overall health. It can benefit people around you too.

And these benefits don't end when your meditation session ends. Meditation can help carry you more calmly through your day.

Meditation and Emotional Well-Being

When you meditate, you can deal more clearly with the information overload that builds up every day and contributes to your stress.

The emotional benefits of meditation can include:

- Gaining a new perspective on stressful situations
- Building skills to manage your stress
- Increasing self-awareness
- Focusing on the present
- Reducing negative emotions
- Increasing imagination and creativity
- Increasing patience and tolerance

Meditation isn't a replacement for traditional medical treatment. But it may be a useful addition to your other treatment.

Mindfulness meditation is based on being mindful, or having an increased awareness and acceptance of living in the present moment. In mindfulness meditation, you broaden your conscious awareness. You focus on what you experience during meditation, such as the flow of your breath. You can observe your thoughts and emotions, but let them pass without judgment.

At the back of the book I've listed some Recommendations if you want to learn more about the wonderful life skill of Mindfulness.

CONCLUSION

My STILL Effect talk prompted this little book, so it is appropriate to ask ourselves why we should be 'still' once in a while?

According to the World Health Organisation, 1 in 4 of us will suffer from some form of mental health issue in our lifetimes. Burnout will be among the world's most prevalent diseases by 2020, joining killers like stroke and diabetes. Stress is a fact of life, arguably a price paid for a life lived well. Do you think you are coping well with it? If you're not, join the club; even the best, brightest, most mentally strong and talented people are sometimes unable to cope. The good news is that we can actively help ourselves to cope with its effects and improve our resiliency skills.

We all do it, leave our needs at the end of the list, after a long day at work, after dinner, after the dishes, after the kids are put to bed...and then, well, we're just too tired, so it can wait until tomorrow. But it can't, it shouldn't, it mustn't, because stress and anxiety don't wait, their effects are immediate, and we need to act straight away to minimise their impact.

Setting a reminder helps. The idea is not to wait until you are stressed, but to make them a habit, a kind of oasis that you visit on a regular basis to 'top up'. So, try them when you are *not* stressed, so they will come to you more naturally when you are stressed.

But we have to start somewhere, right? So, for now, let's focus on the small steps I've given you so you can immediately reduce those stress hormones. Call them mindful moments, oxygen breaks, 'me' time, whatever suits you.

These little breaks are about giving your mind a chance to recover from the conceptual state of 'doing' that we experience on a daily basis, when we are concerned mainly with accomplishing tasks as quickly and efficiently as possible. A mindful break, however, pushes your mind into more of a 'being' state. This state gives your mind a chance to simply 'be', to be still.

Most of us are in an active and occupied state but not necessarily aware of ourselves, others or our environment. The perceptual state on the other hand, is one of observation and opening up our awareness beyond the tasks in front of us. The benefits of allowing our brains small, regular breaks from 'doing' are numerous: our brain is re-energized, our mind is more focused and clear, our body is more relaxed, and we break the spell of thinking we need to be 'doing' all the time.

While mindful breaks are easy to do, they are also just as easy to forget. So here are a few ways to remind yourself.

- Set an alarm on your phone (as often as you feel necessary but at least hourly).
- Put a sticker on your phone or computer or watch or mirror so that every time you look, you are reminded to be still and do one of these activities.

Find out what works best for you. Remember, every time you practice mindfulness, you create more neural connections, making it easier and easier to find your focus and clarity whenever you need it.

I wish all of you good mental health and hope that you have found something in this little book, no matter how small, that will help you to take care of yourselves a little better.

END NOTES:
My favourite apps to download and continue your
mindfulness journey...

- **Headspace**
- **Smiling Mind**
- **Insight Timer**
- **Calm**

Gratitude
This book could not have happened without the love and support
of my husband (and editor) Mark. Thanks also to Dr Gill Hicks
MA MBE, Karen Gunton who taught me all there is to know
about self-publishing and to all the TEDxAdelaide team for their
encouragement and love of new ideas.

Printed in Great Britain
by Amazon

75081509R00058